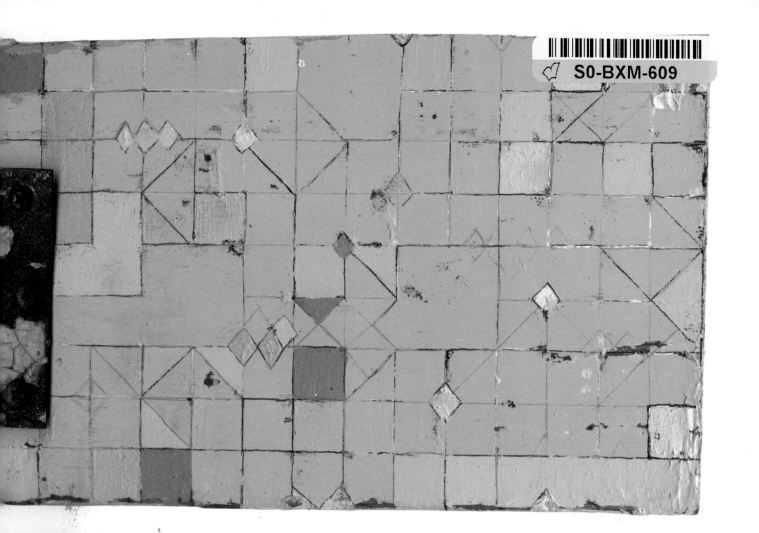

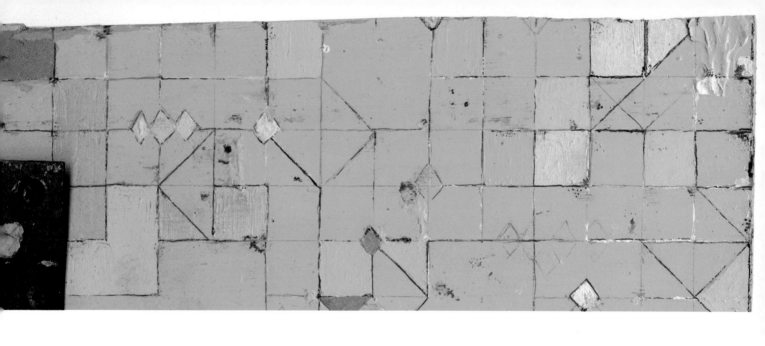

Endpapers, First and Last Page
Kasper Haight

Graphic Design and Layout
Ryan Thompson, Caleb Beyers

www.anteism.com
www.thenumber.biz
www.fantanstudios.com

Production:
thenumber
1-625 Hillside Ave
Victoria, BC V8T 1Z1
Canada

Printed in China
ISBN 0-9782351-0-X

To stay informed about new titles and new projects
please join the mailing list at www.thenumber.biz, or at
www.anteism.com, or write to
P.O. Box 5313
Victoria, BC V8R 6S4
Canada

Acknowledgements:
For unflagging support and patience, we would like to thank
Jamie Allen, Jim Gauer, Casey Woo, Niels and Chris Nohr, Patti
Chiappini, Doris Chung, Josh Miller, Cosmo and Leah Meens,
Matt and Luke, Shawn O'Keefe, Harley Smart, Bill and Kirsten,
Aimster, Luke Ramsey, Piers and Nick, Sam Jones, Shane
Devereaux, Matt Moravec, The Community Arts Council of
Greater Victoria.

theMAKE

of two thousand limited edition copies

Foreword

Bill Cowen

Art movements can not be made, they must develop on their own. Not because they cannot be consciously manipulated through enough hard work, but because movements are organic, and will resist if pushed in any direction. They are eminently flexible, and may be passionate, poor, inconsistent, over analyzed, potentially lucrative and invariably - exploited in their own ways, but always they are collective, collaborative and defy definition -- even to the people who are right inside them. An art movement cannot be designed, nor can it be assembled the way a cobbler crafts a boot. This is because Art movements are prone to growth, and quickly outstrip any abstract plans that may have been made for them. Instead, they follow only the rhythms of their artists, and thrive on whatever inspires their own particular brand of creative vigour.

These things are true, at least of the movement with which I am most intimately familiar, one which is occuring all around me, here in Downtown Victoria, BC in the year 2006. And though at the moment , it seems to have no formal structure, nor any clearly outstanding features to define its essential character, having watched it evolve over the last two years, I believe it is finally time for someone to point out what is going on in the neighbourhood.

With the luxury of hindsight perhaps, I would be able to give an explanation of who started it, and how it was born, what it is up to, and where it might be going. Yet this movement is still writing its history, making it all the more difficult to articulate its nature, never mind its future. As far as i can tell, it began co-incidentally, and has continued passively, gaining much of its momentum without effort, and sustaining itself through a pleasant demeanour as well as a large dose of collaborative good will. With a philosophy of inclusion at its core, its emergence has been the result of many independent minds all working out the next steps, even though its direction is unclear.

Deep existential questions could be asked - - What is actually going on here? Is it really as significant as it seems, or is it happeing everywhere else too, all at the same time? Should it remain a secret, or could it use the exposure? Perhaps it is better not to ask these things. Perhaps the best thing to do, is simply to continue what we are doing anyway, regardless of whether or not anyone has answers. Attend one of the exhibits, better yet, become part of one, and the reasons for doing so become self-evident. Yet still, as an important part of any movement worth its salt is documentation, so there must be at least some attempt made to probe its personality as well as its potential...

That is why this book you are holding exists. It is an attempt to show, if not explain, an art movement as it emerges...

"I think these shows are great because they bring people together, and they just show how many amazing artists there are in Victoria. There are a lot of artists who just keep to themselves and don't really show their work to many other people, but then one of these shows comes along, then all of a sudden they're in it, and then they're doing more shows and stuff, and its amazing".

- Luke Ramsey, Nov 2006

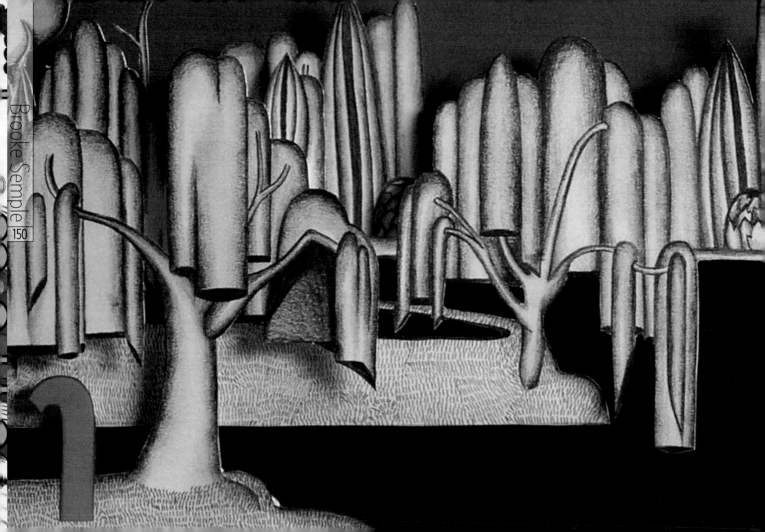

150

THE END OF THE WORLD IS NEAR!

Try not to let your more fanatical side take over.

AS SEEN ON TV

666

People are rarely as good as they might be.

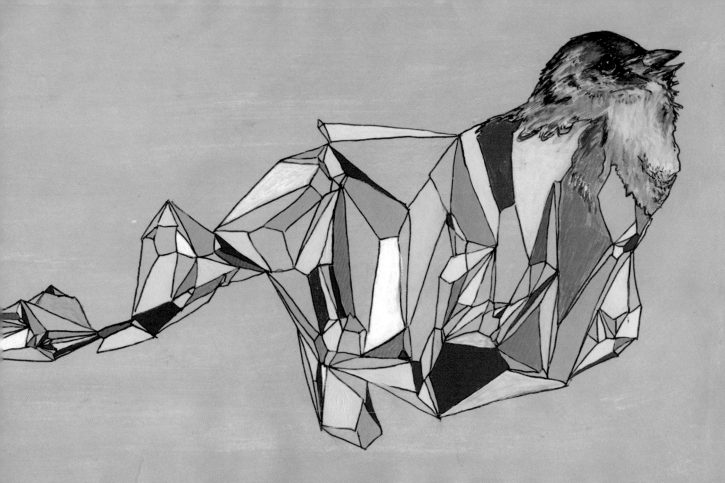

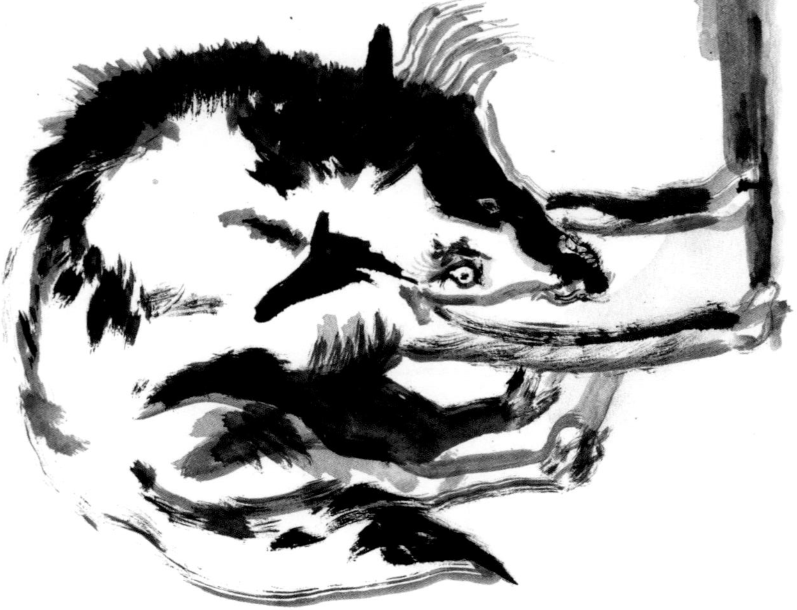

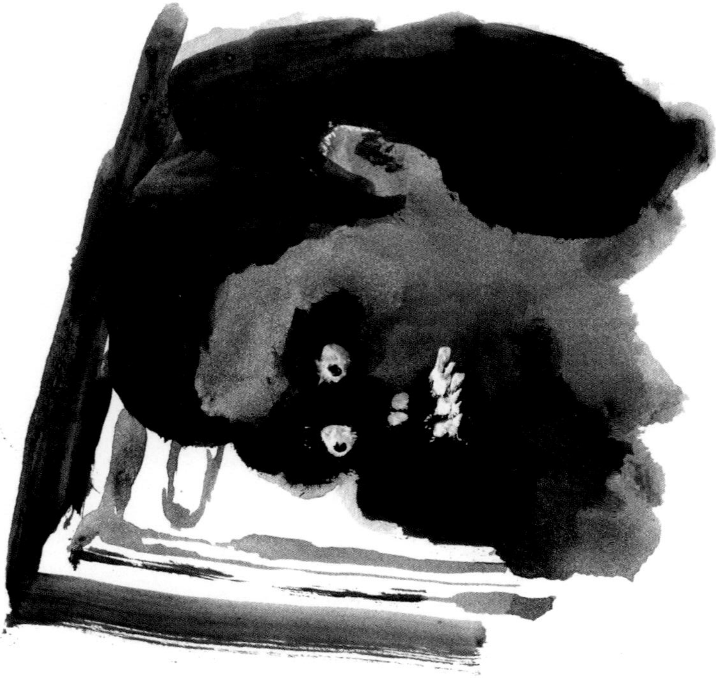

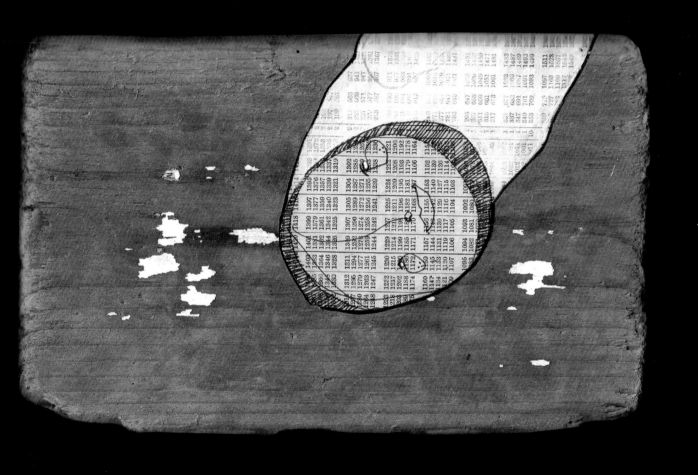

OUDS

PHOTO-GRAPHY PAYS OFF!

QUESTION:

ANSWER:

darkness of WAR

ain't
what
it ~~~~ to be
to be

Way

S and
med
mns

More
than
enough

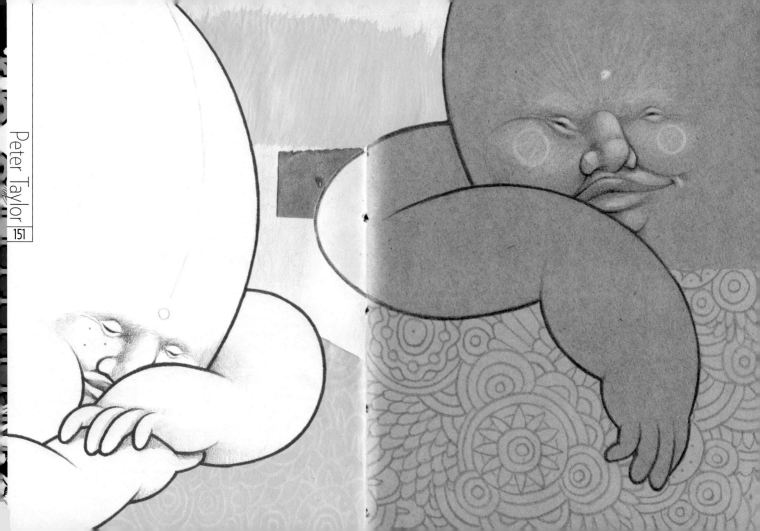

OFF
SH—
ER
AS
TH
A
RIEF.

RIES
FF.

.pArtment 13. R oom 13teen. APT

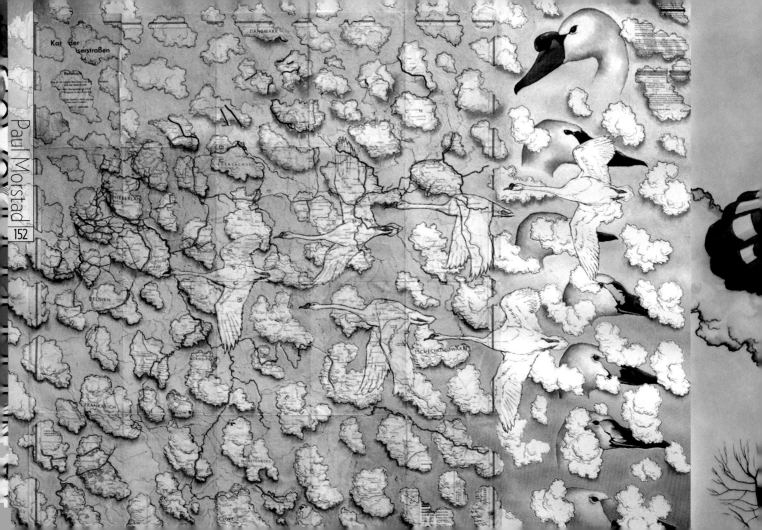

152

152

THE DEATH POEM (ABRIDGED)

DEATH COMES WITH A STORY THAT'S NEVER BEEN TOLD.   DEATH COMES IN SLOW AND ROMANCES THE OLD.

BY HANK PINE ESQ.

DEATH COMES BY AND CRASHES EVERY PARTY IT ATTENDS.

DEATH COMES AND TAKES AWAY ALL MY FRIENDS.

DEATH COMES AND LEAVES A SWEET, SICKLY SCENT.

DEATH COMES AND STAYS LIKE A FART IN A TENT.

DEATH COMES FOR WORMS IN THE SHAPE OF BIRDS.

WHEN DEATH COMES, IT LEAVES ME AT A LOSS FOR WORDS.

EGAN

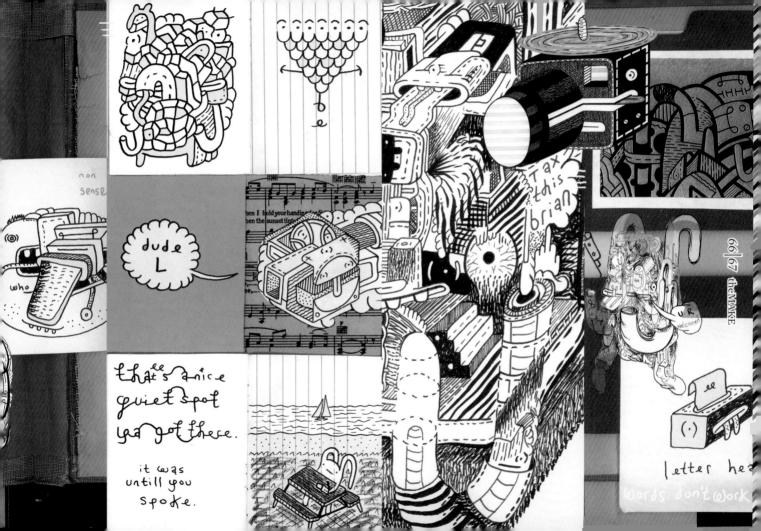

driver beware

Hebron, Palestine. 2006.

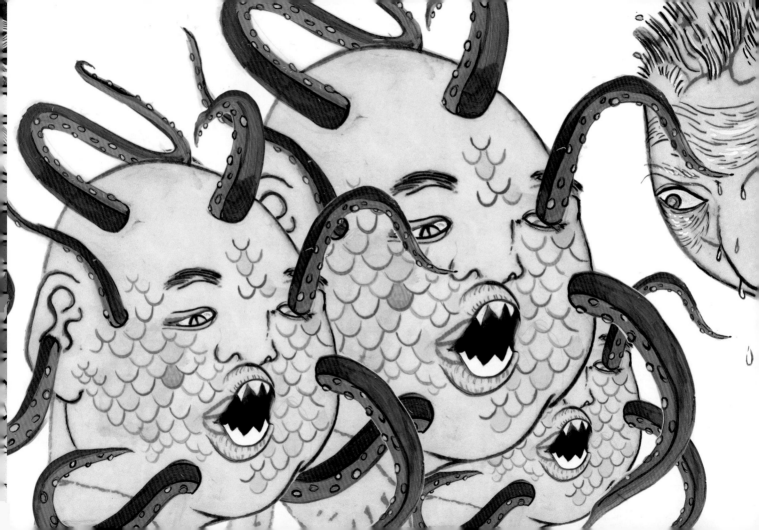

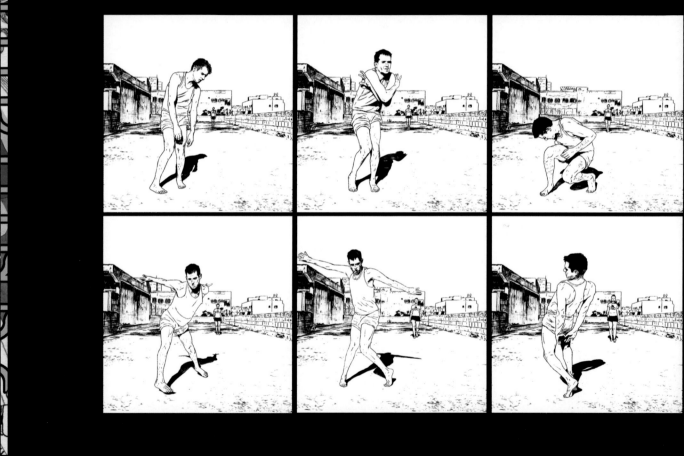

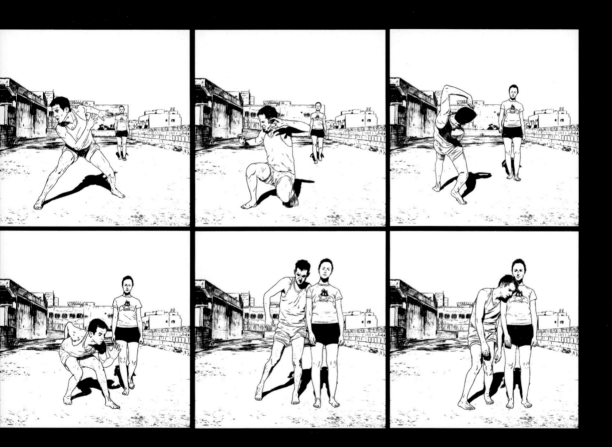

The Hovering Gentlemen's Club

marc johns

marc johns

ever wonder

NEW

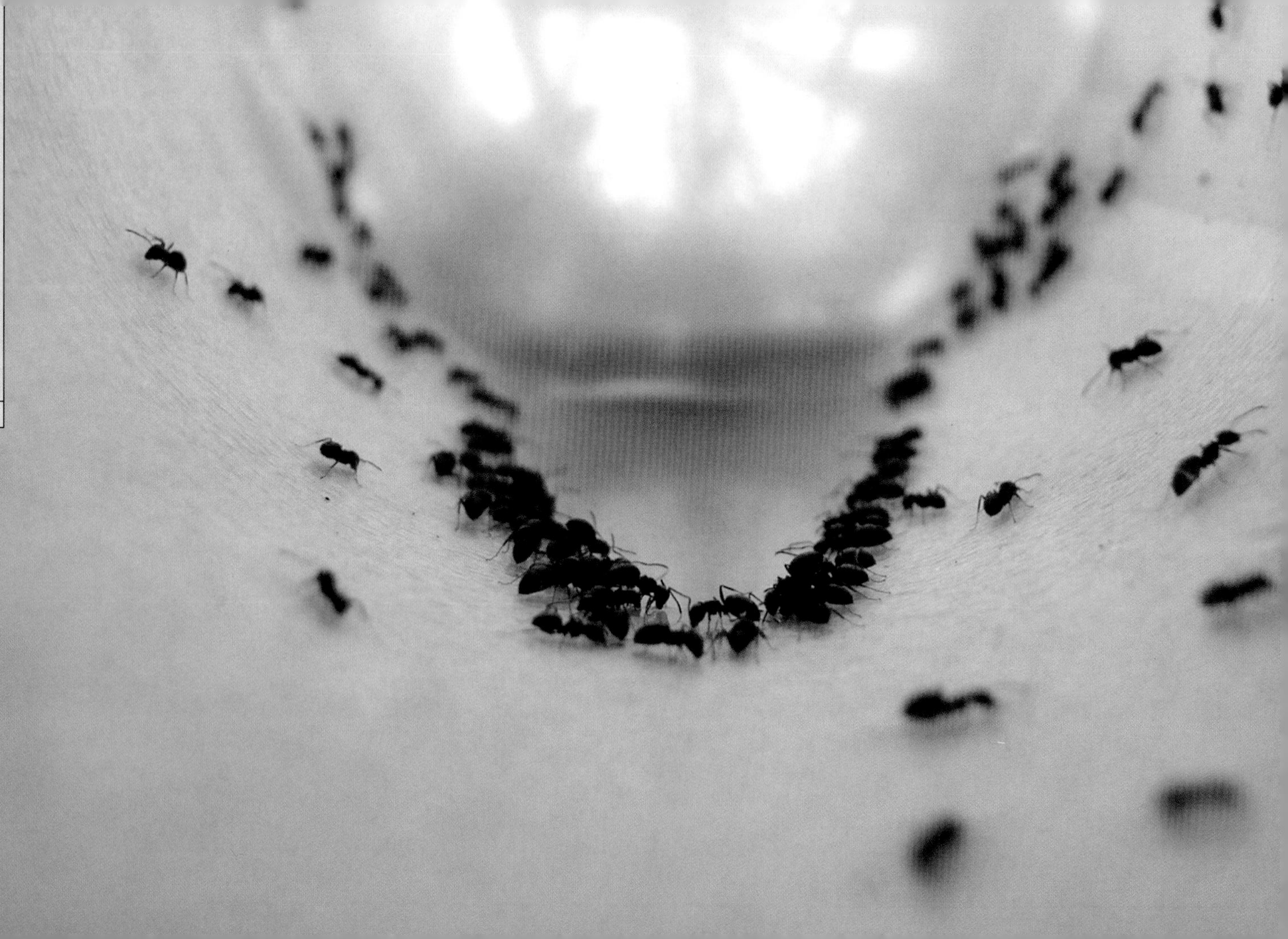

Geoffrey Tomlin-Hood

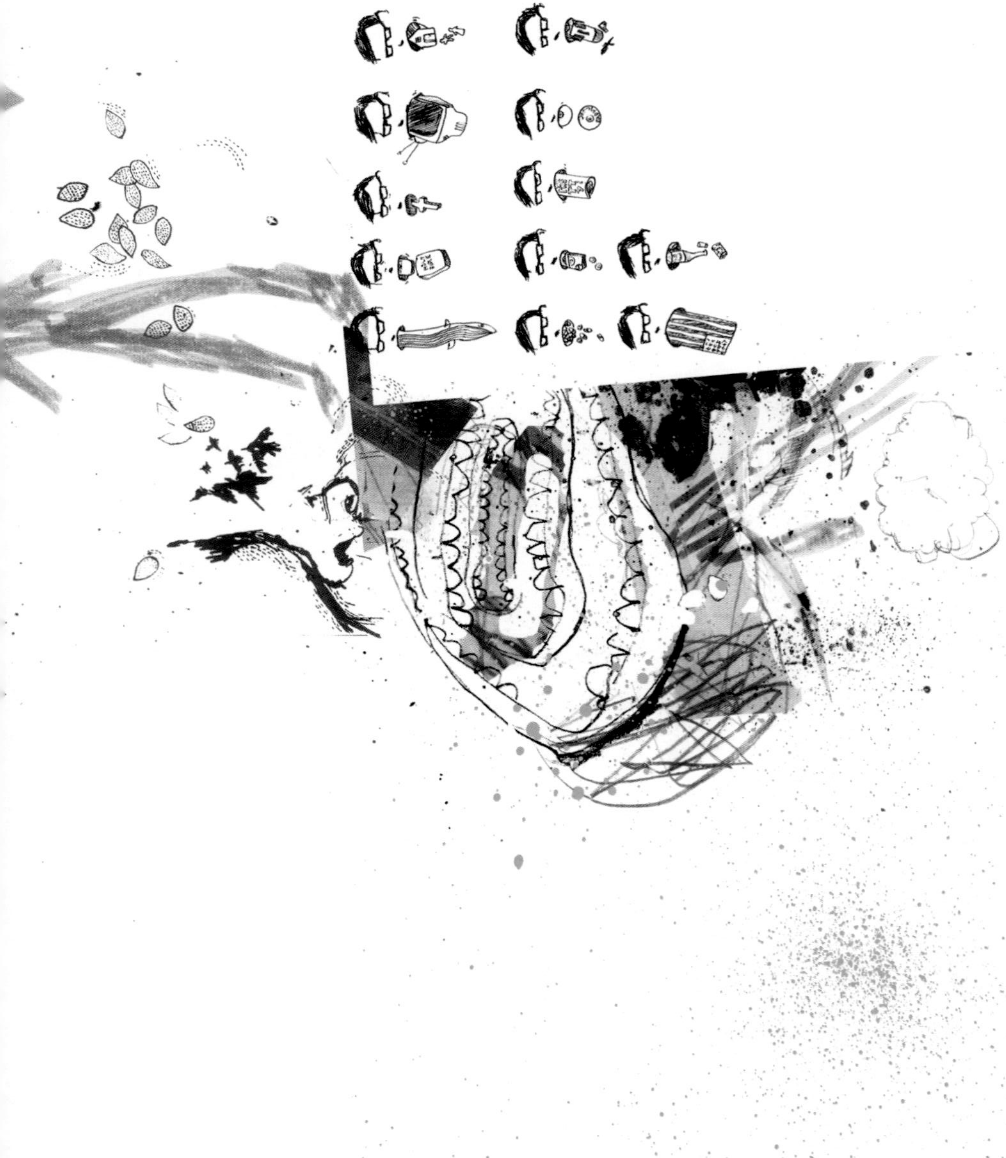

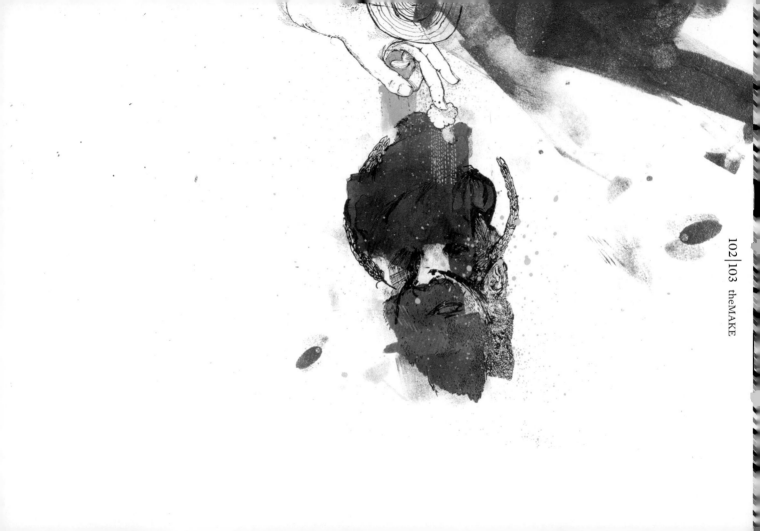

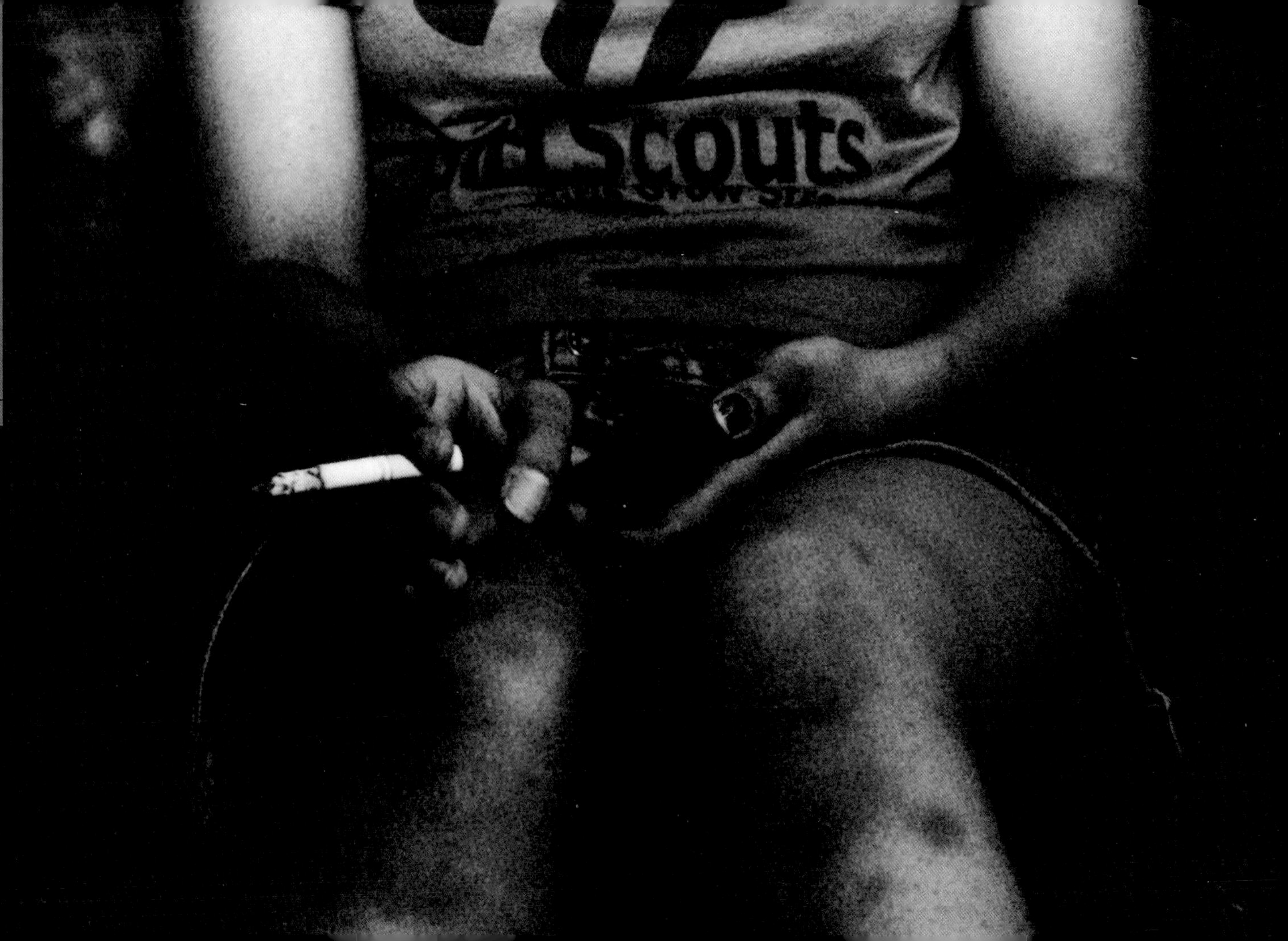
Scouts

Hero Make-Up .

OCT 0 6 2006

Woodpile

COLLECTIVE

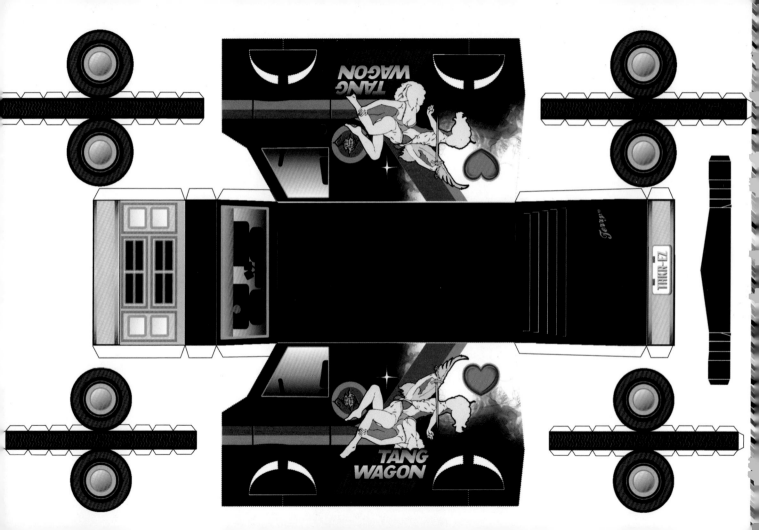

there are no instructions.

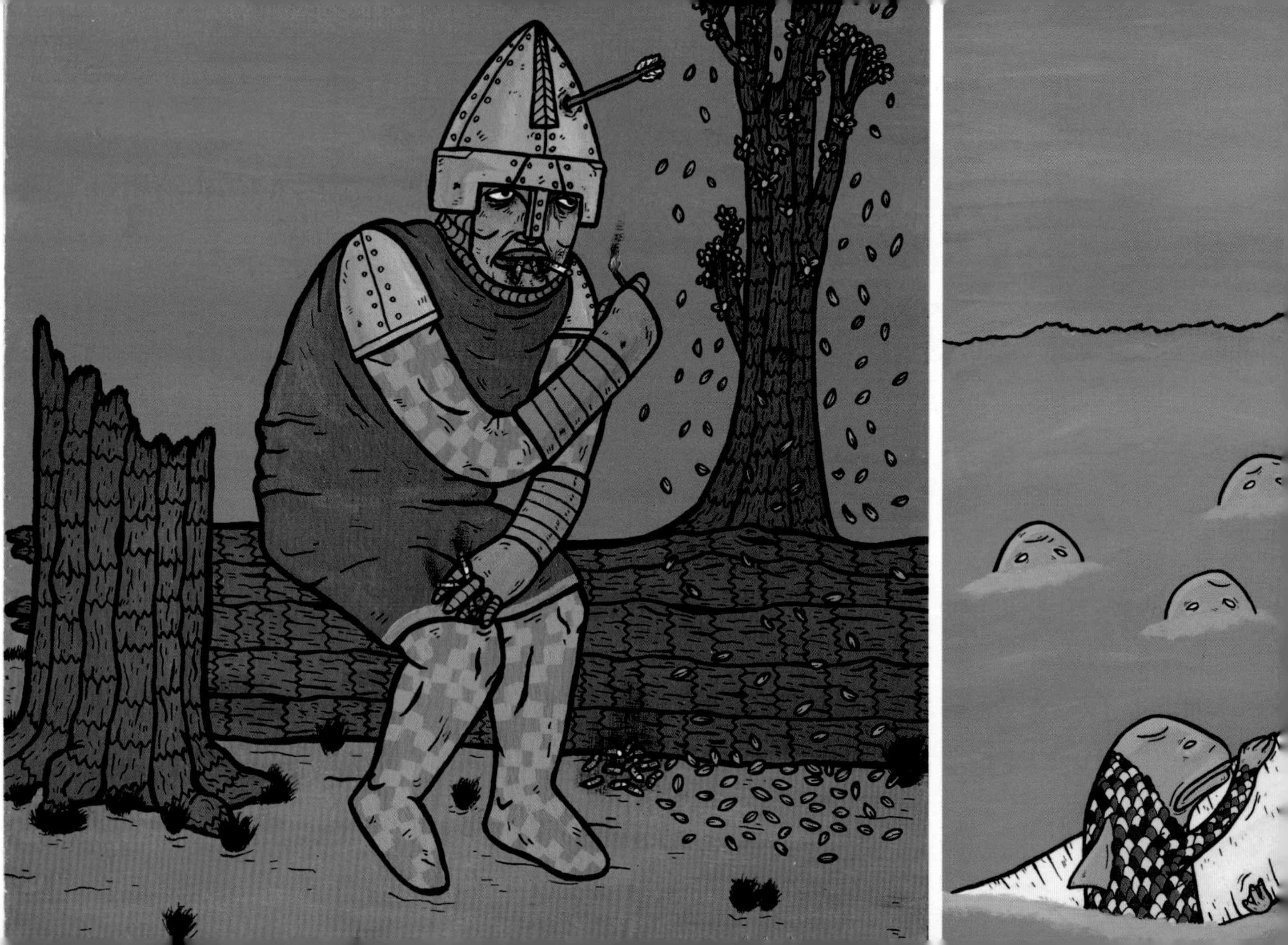

I AWOKE TO A CONSTANT

SCRATCHING NOISE.

AND IT WAS VERY LATE.

THE NIGHT AIR

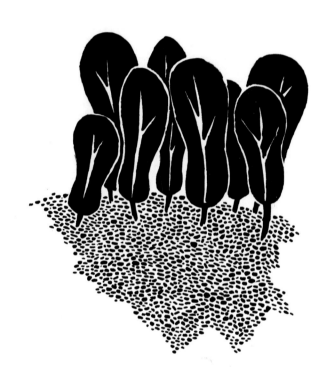

WAS COOL ON MY BELLY.

I RESPONDED
WITH 4000
MESSAGES.

...AND THEN
MANY MORE

AN ENDLESS STREAM
OF WORDS ACROSS
THE OCEAN.

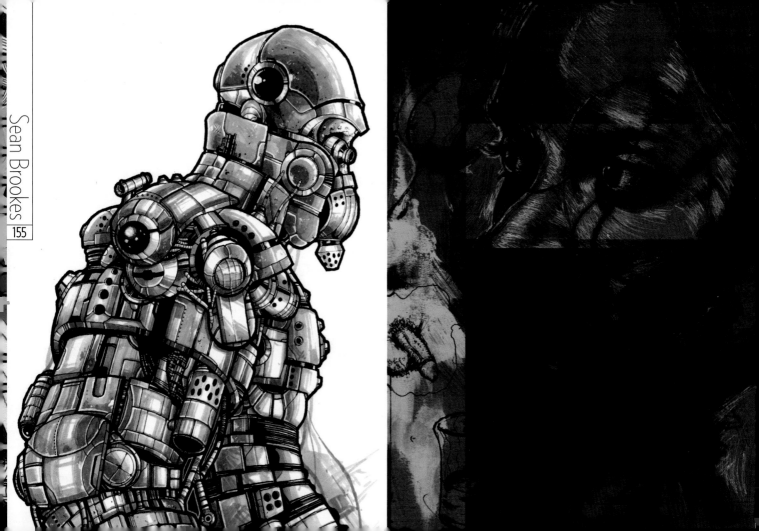

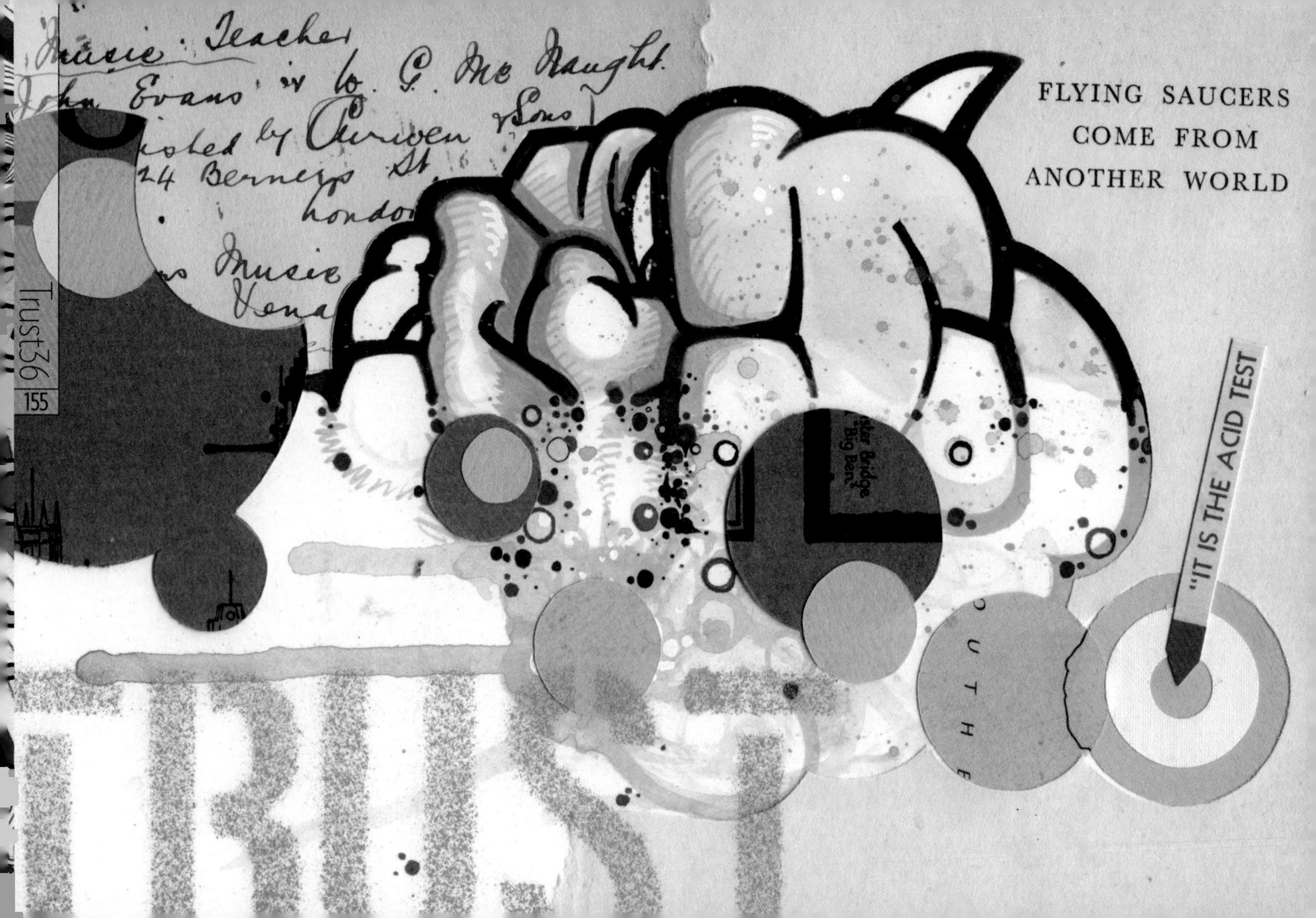

Music Teacher
John Evans iv to G. Mc Naught.
...isted by Chriven & Sons
24 Berners St.
London
...s Music
Vena

FLYING SAUCERS
COME FROM
ANOTHER WORLD

"IT IS THE ACID TEST

...ster Bridge
"Big Ben"

UTHE

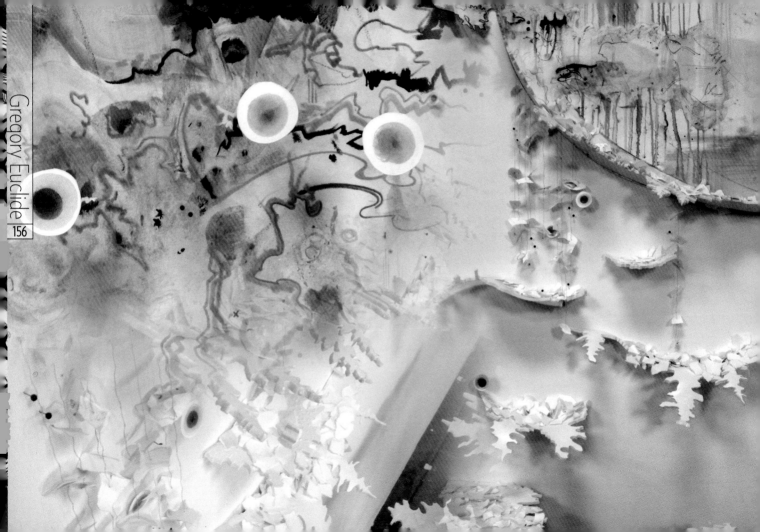

156

280 permanent marker

JUMBO WASHABLE

EXTRA BROAD PERMANENT MARKER

Pentel
chisel point
PERMANENT MARKER
MADE IN CHINA

HI-TEXT
MAXI MARKER 840
PERMANENT MARKER

ZEBRA
McKie
EXTRA BOLD oil base

STAEDTLER
Lumocolor

JUMBO

MARKER
10 mm
Mellow POP

EXPO
DRY ERASE

ARTISTS:

For information about the artwork depicted in this book, please contact the artists.

The Nohr Gentlemen

The Nohr Gentlemen have recently expanded into another generation, and remain of sound mind and good heart. They care about creativity, and its pursuit in all fields. They share a respect and outward appreciation for those around them, and create wonder in their wake.

Chris: chris@techimp.biz
Niels: admin@realfoto.com

Chew Malimine

Matthew Feyld, Saskatoon based artist, is a lad who grew up with a birth defect that made his head swell unbelieveably. This happened at the worst times possible: during show and tell, at the science fair, on his first date... It happened from stress. He found that keeping calm helped his head stay normal and drawing, painting, and scribbling were his cures. It recreates his greatest fears... Beady eyed monsters with giant ballon heads fighting off the world in tights.

www.flickr.com/photos/driftwould
business_attire@hotmail.com

Brooke Semple

brookesemple@hotmail.com

Ryan Thompson

Ryan Thompson's work is the amalgamation of collage into photography. Using his camera like a scalpel to slice imagery from the world around him. Typography, texture, and popular imagery are cropped then layered in a ghostly fashion. Multiple exposures combine fractured versus, abstract imagery with a detectable underlying subject. Each photo is an exploration of time and remembrance. Looking into the imagery slowly reveals new concepts and changing opinions. A meditative process of recognition, recollection and reflection.

ryan@anteism.com

Tamsyn Dennis

Collage is like a sickness. You are always seeking bits and pieces, cutting them out, saving them in neverending piles of images and text. I am often surprised by the results of gleaning from my collections- what has attracted my attention, and the themes that quickly develop. I also love mail art, and making zines. To get some snail mail email me. (say that three times fast!)

thisandorthat@gmail.com

Caitlin Gallupe

caitlin.gallupe@gmail.com

Shea Moir

164 lbs of wrestlemania. Making artwork until he reaches heavyweight wrestle poundage. Currently injury free. Dislikes border crossings. Toyota burrito van owner. Good listener. Has walked across the Mississippi river with other tourists. Allergies include substances containing urushol.

sheapony@yahoo.com

Caleb Beyers

Caleb Beyers was born in Cheltenham, England in 1982 to South African draft dodging parents. He spent his early days running around naked on a small Island off the West Coast of Canada before he packed up and looked around. He now lives in Victoria, and likes to play with anything that can make a picture. His drawings have appeared in The Walrus Magazine, Swift Magazine, The Harvard Lampoon, and he's made videos with Red Bull, Oakley Denim, Immaculate Machine, and Neko Case.

www.thenumber.biz
caleb.beyers@gmail.com

P. Williams

My paintings are fun, and they are supposed to be fun, but they are also intended to be challenging. In many ways, my work functions like a comic, drawing heavily on the lexicon of comic mechanisms, but also invents, distorts, and leaves few puzzles for the viewer to discover. The paintings can be viewed as single panels, or as a collection of snapshots of some novel, standing perfectly alone yet some how complete.

www.pwilliamsart.com
pwilliamsart@yahoo.com

Jaret Penner

Jaret Penner (1976) lives and works in Port Moody, BC Canada. He is a member of the Vancouver art collective Humanfive since 2001. As well he plays music with instrumental post-rock shoegazer ensemble, the Precious Fathers and rock n' roll pioneers, the Battles.

His eye-catching drawings and paintings have a visibly spontaneous style which creates a strong visual impact thanks to his simple but refined detailing.

Jaret has shown his art internationally as well he has been recently featured in the acclaimed Tiny Vices group show at Spencer Brownstone Gallery, New York, and in various publications such as Dose, BC Business and Only Magazine, plus a series of selfmade books and zines.

www.humanfive.com
jaretpenner@hotmail.com

Ty Danylchuk

No contact information available.

Fumi Nakamura

Fumi Minnie Nakamura born in Shimizu-Shizuoka, Japan 1984. She moved to the United States at the age of 11 and has been living in Bay Area, California for almost 10 years. She attended: California College of Arts and Crafts, San Francisco Art Insititute, and San Jose State University for various studies and to practice her skills. She mostly self-taught herself and from books.

www.miniminiaturemouse.com
contact@miniminiaturemouse.com

Eric Chan

My work straddles the fine line between art/design and technology. Having interest in exploring the intersections of art and technology, my illustrations are composed by generative programs that I have developed.

Beautiful, detailed and chaotic are words that describe the nature of my pieces -most heavily influenced by Japanese print, graffiti and music.

I have won several awards, including the 2006 Flash in the Can Award Best Canadian Student and the 2005 Macromedia Student Innovation Award and have appeared in a variety of publishing mediums, from the design/graffiti magazine Beautiful Decay to online webzines including Germany-based Encore Magazine.

http://eepmon.com
kilo.pixel@gmail.com

Caleb Speller

I live in Canada
I live in Victoria B.C.
I make art here everyday
I take pictures of what I can't draw
I draw what I can't paint
I paint what I can't see
I write what I can't picture

www.elephantante.com
caleb_speller@yahoo.ca

Matt Cipov

www.mattcipov.com

Amy Bonner

No contact information available.

Jamie Allen

Jamie Allen is a world traveller. She has visited over 40 countries in Europe, Asia, and North America. She takes pictures of the things she sees, and isn't afraid to wade into thoroughly unfamiliar surroundings.

jamie_m_allen@hotmail.com

Randy Laybourne

www.lookforwardtothepast.com
info@lookforwardtothepast.com

Pete Taylor

Raised on the small British Columbia island town of Quadra. Peter now resides in Vancouver where you can find him drawing, or painting, riding his bike, or practicing yoga. With no formal artistic training Peter's art has progressed with patients and practice.

www.handmadefeat.com
peter@handmadefeat.com

Lyle Schultz

cactusjournals@yahoo.ca

Paul Morstad

Paul Morstad is an animator for the National Film Board of Canada. He makes marvellous pictures of all types of animals, all types of bottles, and all types of music.

www.paulmorstad.com
paulmorstad@gmail.com

Jenny Ritter

jennycomics.blogspot.com

Reanna Adler

Reanna Alder won the Amphibian and Reptile Keeper's Association colouring contest when she was eight, but had to give the prize to her brother because he was the one who wanted to go in the first place.
She has since made drawings for posters, camp t-shirts, Voiceworks magazine, and the cover of This Side of West. She has a BFA in Creative Writing from the University of Victoria. Her piece on pages 58 &59 is called

"One of several possible ways to redeem the cumshot." You could figure out a way to contact her if you really wanted to.

Hank Pine

Hank Pine thinks about death a lot, yes, and resides on a large island off the western coast of Canada. He is also one half of the travelling-vaudevillianshowcase, "HANK PINE and LILY FAWN".

www.hankandlily.com.

Mike Egan

When I look at my paintings, I think about the last four years of working within funeral homes. There are three main themes that run through my paintings, which include: Religion, Life and Death. Funerals are the perfect way to celebrate all three at the same time. I feel like I'm painting people's funerals a lot of the times. Whether it's their religious beliefs or their manner of death, I like to pay tribute to the people who have passed on.

e-mail- egan159@yahoo.com
website- www.eganpaintings.com

Luke Ramsey

Luke Ramsey has exhibited his work in Vancouver, Seattle, Portland, Los Angeles, Denver, Montreal, Rochester, Philadelphia, Baltimore, Sweden, Taiwan and Tokyo. Luke has created an artist residency with his partner Angela, called Islands Fold. They publish small press books and zines and invite artists to the residency free of charge.

www.islandsfold.com

Colin MacRea

I have been creating metal structures from my drawings since 1999.i have been fortunate to come across a process and create a style that constantly keeps me stimulated and inspired. I am forever sourcing out material, reclaiming old barn roofs and siding, finding old industrial sights and scrapyards to seek out the used and forgotten with intent to re-work it into an uncommon form. The piece in this book: "along the way from here to there" was comissioned for Neil Young. It was a slight departure from my usual lines and content. This is the canadien prairies in all its beauty and splendour.extreme seasonal contrasts play out under a never ending skyline that parallels the rolling feilds.history leaves a trail still travelled with all its man-made landmarks along the way. Who doesn't love an old steam train. Now that's pure romance...

www.colinmacraeart.com

david parsons

Among david's experiences in the West Bank, the hospitality of the Palestinians stands out as truly remarkable; not casual hospitality under idyllic circumstances, but the genuine hospitality of a people who survive daily under military occupation. He remains humbly thankful for this kindness.

dpphoto.ca
yahoodotca@hotmail.com

Noah Becker

My recent involvement with painting is in expanding the narrative. Researching Flemish artists Pieter Bruegel and Hieronymus Bosch's intricate pictures began this process. The narrative is surprisingly contemporary considering the picture was painted in 1559. Studying Flemish Proverbs has guided my process towards the invention of unconventional contemporary images entitled Realms. These complex works combine elements from pop culture, art history and the imagination. Reinventing ways in which source material is used has become an important part of my process. Realms are about the state of different worlds seen through the lens of art history, popular culture and dream experience.

www.noahbecker.org

Kevin Silver

humanocinco@gmail.com

Ben VanNetten

Photography by: Ben van Netten and Keira Pinchbeck.

Ben van Netten and Keira Pinchbeck live in victoria B.C. Canada. Where they make photos for the amusement of there friends and relatives. They are currently building a multibillion dollar photographic empire which the UN says is the biggest threat to world peace since the invention of the hydrogen bomb.

www.benvannetten.com

Howie Tsui

Ho Yan (Howie) Tsui was born on January 19, 1978 in Hong Kong. Several months later, he and his mother rejoined their family in Lagos, Nigeria. During these nascent years, Howie: a) went on safaris in Kenya, b) got a concussion on the London Bridge, c) confronted ghosts in a haunted hotel in Manilla, and d) during a near-fatal high fever, had hallucinations of ceiling-piercing rain that showered upon apparitions of Disney characters. In 1983, his family immigrated to Thunder Bay, Ontario, where he began his assimilation into western culture through street hockey and heavy metal music. Tsui's 'suspended adolescent' artistic approach is informed by such experiences. Tsui received his BFA in 2002 from the University of Waterloo and is currently painting and illustrating in Ottawa, Canada.,

www.howietsui.com
themongrel @ howietsui.com

Ruth Gwily

My name is Ruth Gwily I am an artist/illustrator working and living in Tel-aviv, Israel. I studied graphic design and illustration in Bezalel academy for art and design in Jerusalem. but i work only as an illustrator. My work is being published regularly in news-papers and magazines in Israel and beyond. I have recently published an anthology of my work in Paris.

ruthgwily@yahoo.com
ruthgwily.com

Ric Stultz

www.ricstultz.com

Marc Johns

Marc Johns creates drawings of hesitant gentlemen, grumpy beasts, and miscellaneous oddities. These characters are confused about their identities. They are trying on labels with mixed results. They are searching for meaning, unable to draw any conclusions.

Marc grew up in the Eastern Townships of Quebec. He received his B.A. from Bishop's University, where he completed a double major in Fine Arts (studio), and Business (what was he thinking?). He draws - a lot. He's been drawing since he was tiny. He's not tiny anymore, but he's not exactly very big either.

draw.vox.com
marcjohns.com.

Whitney Davis

In no particular order I present the top 15 things that I still do, for which I still feel no remorse [for the most part]: 1 live with my parents (during my extended visits to Victoria); 2 drink cans of PBR, front shrewd attitude & badger strangers; 3 blare punk and rap while cruising the interstates in my 86 Volvo; 4 paint big pictures; 5 love jimmy buffet; 6 accept inane manual labor jobs for minimum wage in order to ride my snowboard everyday; 7 overtly stare at hot dudes; 8 win at foosball;

9 wear knee-highs or long-johns; 10 am a photographer at summer camp; 11 am proud to be an American/am proud to be a Canadian; 12 sleepover at my friend's houses; 13 call home collect; 14 lose my wallet/passports/ credit cards on a regular basis; 15 cherish the jobs that allow me to be outside all year long.

whitneyherrick@gmail.com

Charlotte Campbell

Currently lives and works in Victoria B.C. Creates paintings using pen and pencil drawings incorporated with screenprinted layers. Her images often sprout from natural forms and animals. She also takes these ideas further into her sculpture and clothing design practice.

eyecheewawa@hotmail.com

Silja Götz

Born in Regensburg, Germany in 1974. Studied Communication Design at the GSO Fachhochschule, Nürnberg, Germany. Graduated in 1998 with self-edited audiobook "Abenteuer des Alltags". January 1999 to April 2001: Work as designer and Illustrator for Allegra Magazine, Hamburg. June 2001: Move to Madrid/ Spain and work as a freelance illustrator.
www.siljagoetz.com
silja@siljagoetz.com

Geoffrey Tomlin-Hood

Geoffrey Tomlin-Hood's work has appeared in HauteDoll, The international Doll Quarterly, Dollz Mania, The Paper Doll review and Dream of Doll. His home base is in Kalutara, Sri Lanka but he works out of the southern capital of Colombo.

geoff@thenumber.biz

Brandon Velestuk

Brandon lives in victoria bc and has been for 3 years. In the winter time, his hands feel cold more often than not. He feels strange writing in the third person.

www.thedirton.com
www.sixsidedocean.com

Matt Moravec

Matt Moravec, known occasionally as "Giraffe," lives in New York city where he runs around taking pictures, making friends, and otherwise keeping it real. He has a dog named "Scooter" who likes to ride in his tote bag. He takes photographs every day, and is never in lacking ideas, or in wanting to storm the universe.

mattmoravec@gmail.com

Matt Cipov

www.mattcipov.com

Woodpile Collective

Simultaneous collaborations & unplanned paintings between founding members: Shawn O'Keefe, Blythe Hailey & Sean McLaughlin.

Our evolving process continues to shift from painting to painting... Instead of becoming familiar with a certain formula or outcome we find ourselves sitting for long periods of time when we have completed a piece...looking back into it... discovering it's diversity...as though we hadn't seen it before. Each painters state of mind, emotion and level of participation in a piece pulls the dynamics in certain direction... landscapes & portraits...graffiti & abstract impression...Aerosol and Oil... all find a place in the Woodpile set.... sometimes in one painting.

www.woodpile.ca

Studio 16 1/2

Hidden in the Bowels of Victoria's Chinatown, Studio 16 1/2 supports creative projects such as this *5 day Mural* among local artists. see website for details ...

www.fantanstudios.com
info@fantanstudios.com

Ehren Salazar

Ehren Salazar was born in 1979 and raised in Vancouver, in and around Queen Elizabeth park. He runs a gallery now, on Main and 26th called Little Mountain Studios (formerly inhabited by the Butchershop Collective) in Vancouver B.C., with Ryan Anderson, Nathan Drillot, and

Alex Cieslik. Ehren is studying classical animation at the Purple Thissel in Vancouver, as well as researching Vancouver's past at the city archives. Ehren enjoys revisiting RBI baseball on Nintendo, as well as drawing in our Provinces Courtrooms, City Halls, food courts, and coffee shops. Currently Ehren is working on finishing the illustrations to a children's book "The Princess of Bazu" by Peter Salvador, published by Mudscout Media out of Montreal.

www.monsterdinosaur.com
monsterdinosaur@hotmail.com

Caleb Beyers/Trust 36

After only meeting him a few times, Trust gave Caleb a purple hooded sweatshirt with speakers printed all over it. Caleb put it on and was all "look at me, I'm a rapper!" then danced around for a little while. When he was done dancing, he sat down and made some pictures with Trust. The two of them enjoy eachother's company and reckon they'll be making pictures together again soon.

Ben Kehoe

Ben Kehoe is an artist in Pittsburgh. he has been known to frequent bars...lurking in the corner waiting for his chance to perform his signature move...smashing a full bottle of beer against the wall, putting on a fake mustache and sunglasses and then exiting with a no-handed cartwheel blowing into a slide whistle. He does stuff for unicorn mountain, for himself and for his mom. Marne's cat gives him allergies...but she does the opposite."

www.benkehoe.com
ben@benkehoe.com

Max Estes

Max Estes is a artist and author living and working in Milwaukee, Wisconsin, USA. His primary artistic focus is on narrative structures, and the endless possibilities of the comics medium. He received his BFA from the Milwaukee Institute of Art and Design, and is earning his MFA from the University of Wisconsin, Milwaukee. He checks his email far too often.

www.maxestes.com
max@maxestes.com

Basco5

Basco5 is a Street/Fine Artist based out of Vancouver Canada. His artwork has been displayed in galleries and back alleys both locally and internationally. His style has been describe as "Street Bubble Gum" it's cute but also shows a range of feelings such as innocence and pain. He's had his hand in gallery shows, graphic design, clothing, product design, fine art, murals for movies (the L word), street art, and even doll making. He believes very much that artist deserve to making a living from there creativity and often handles most of his own art selling and business.

www.basco5.com
www.flickr.com/photos/basco5/

Chris Von Szombathy

chrisvonszombathy@yahoo.ca

Luke Ramsey/Alex Purdy

Collaboration by Luke Ramsey and

Alex Purdy, courtesy of Island's Fold.

www.graphdrome.com
www.islands fold.com

Shawn O'Keefe

I am an Illustrator, Painter & Graphic artist living & working in Victoria BC Canada. My work lives with me...I have a studio in my basement where you can find me almost everyday...ping ponging between computer workstation, drawing table & easel...unsure of what's coming next...I keep creating...I love what I do.

My wife Susan and our two boys Graeme & Ian make life very fulfilling and bring me sandwiches when "daddy has a deadline".

www.trust36.com
artificialflavour@shaw.ca

Matthew Janicak

Matthew Janicak is from the Chicago area. He has an upcoming feature film: the TMNTijuana Bibles.

janicak@gmail.com

Caleb Beyers & Geoffrey Tomlin-Hood

Caleb and Geoffrey live, but do not sleep together in Victoria, BC. In general, Caleb likes to work, and Geoff likes to party. Occasionally, they party together, occasionally they work together, the partying is not pictured in this book.

Peter Thompson

Peter Thompson was born in London, Ontario, Canada, and is a high school graduate. He didn't like colouring books as a young child, because simply colouring in other peoples drawings wasn't nearly as interesting as drawing his own. While he's experimented with 'paint' and 'collage' over the years, and continues to do so, he considers himself primarily a 'drawer'. He wishes all of you well, or, at least, doesn't wish any of you specific harm.

petey_funnyfeety@yahoo.com

Anteism

Since 2003 Ryan Thompson has been operating an online entity known as Anteism™. He strives to help promote artists while creating links for artist collaborations. The site continues to grow and mature as with the artists that contribute.

Anteism has begun a new project called the "Showcase Series". Selected artists will be showcased on the Anteism website with a gallery and interview. A screen-printed poster of the artist's work is printed to commemorate the showcase.

www.anteism.com
ryan@anteism.com

Harley Smart

b. 1981
From Vancouver Island, BC, currently living in Montreal, Quebec, interning
and freelancing in visual art publishing while studying fine arts at Concordia University.

www.finewest.ca
harleysmart@hotmail.com

Gregory Euclide

Gregory Euclide currently lives in Minneapolis, MN and attends graduate school at the Minneapolis College of Art and Design.

Public Transit: Y
Religion: N
Eggs: Y
Public Parks Y
Winter: Y
Crowds: N
Pine Trees: Y
Murakami: Y
City Planners: N
CCO: Y
NPR: Y
Suburbs: N

www.gregoryeuclide.com
geuclide@gmail.com

Allister Lee

Allister Lee (ALIST) likes collecting black markers. His submitted illustration to theMAKE depicts 24 of his 200 and counting different black ink markers. When not scouring dollar shops, art supply stores and his friends' drawing boxes for new marker specimens on his quest for Guinness Book World Record status, he is busily preparing work for his ongoing Alist Chinatown World Tour.

www.enterthealist.com
alistsays@gmail.com

Kasper Haight

clem_snide_pi@yahoo.ca

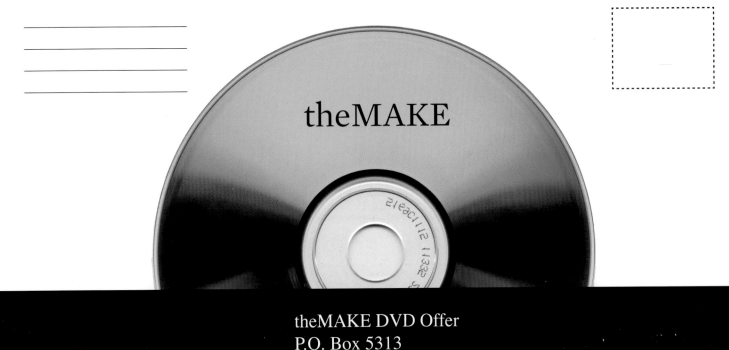

theMAKE

theMAKE DVD Offer
P.O. Box 5313
Victoria, BC V8R 6S4
Canada

If you want to redeem your
theMAKE DVD, complete with
short films, music videos, and
other rarities, please tear out this
page, fill out the following form
completely, apply the appropri-
ate postage, and drop in the mail.

Feel free to decorate.

Name:

Address:

E-mail address:

Thank you for supporting independent publishing. Your patronage means that a new group of artists is one step closer to having their work in the hands of a stranger, potential buyer, potential friend, enemy, collaborator, benefactor, fan, hater, champion, etc. It also means that a new publisher is one step closer to being able to sustain itself and create high-quality books outside of the corporate, market-minded publishing industry.

With your continued help, we will slowly work toward ending the glut of impersonal, ill-conceived, manipulative drivel that currently clogs newsstands and bookstore shelves all over the world. Each artist in this book has taken the time, free from the constraints of the traditional publishing system, to share their personal vision, and communicate some part of their world view. We hope you enjoy your book for years to come, pass it along to your friends, and seek to find your own forms of expression.

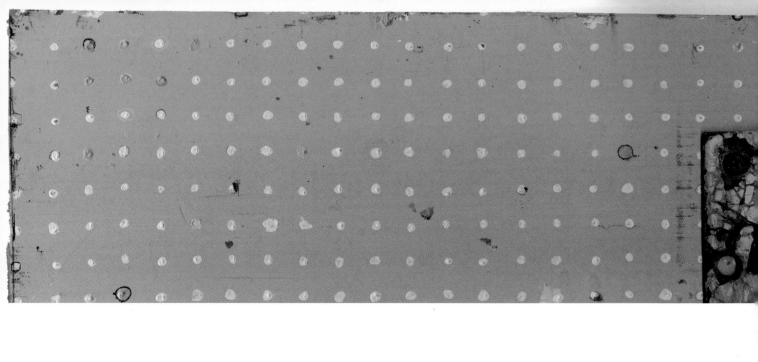

all images © credited artists

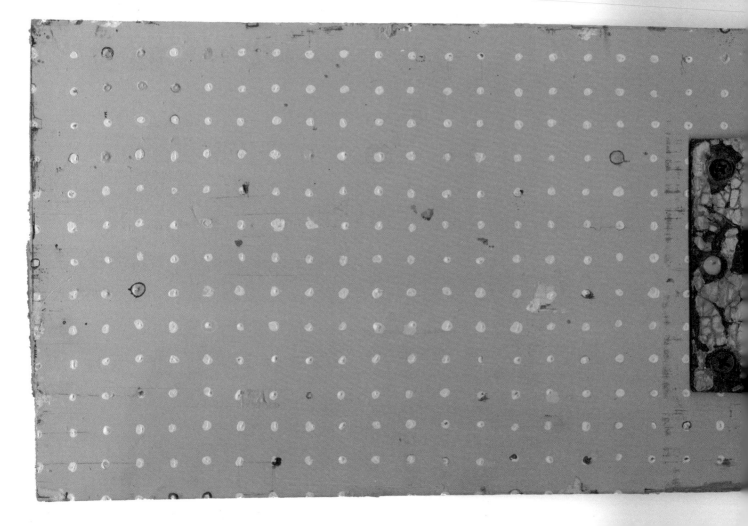